PASSIVE INCOME

Explore Proven Methods That Help to Bring You a
Passive Flow of Money

(A Guide to Making Money Online by Facebook
Advertising)

Heidi Neihoff

Published by Andrew Zen

Heidi Neihoff

All Rights Reserved

Passive Income: Explore Proven Methods That Help to Bring You a Passive Flow of Money (A Guide to Making Money Online by Facebook Advertising)

ISBN 978-1-77485-153-1

Legal & Disclaimer

The information contained in this book is not designed to replace or take the place of any form of medicine or professional medical advice. The information in this book has been provided for educational and entertainment purposes only.

The information contained in this book has been compiled from sources deemed reliable, and it is accurate to the best of the Author's knowledge; however, the Author cannot guarantee its accuracy and validity and cannot be held liable for any errors or omissions. Changes are periodically made to this book. You must consult your doctor or get professional medical advice before using any of the suggested remedies, techniques, or information in this book.

Upon using the information contained in this book, you agree to hold harmless the Author from and against any damages, costs, and expenses, including any legal fees potentially resulting from the application of any of the information provided by this guide. This disclaimer applies to any damages or injury caused by the use and application, whether directly or indirectly, of any advice or information presented, whether for breach of contract, tort, negligence, personal injury, criminal intent, or under any other cause of action.

You agree to accept all risks of using the information presented inside this book. You need to consult a professional medical practitioner in order to ensure you are both able and healthy enough to participate in this program.

Table of Contents

Introduction

This report provides many options for passive income generation. While some opportunities require capital investment, others will only require time and effort.

Passive income can be used to make more time with your family, friends, and even travel the world.

Passive income is an income that doesn't require any ongoing effort to maintain. Your passive income business should be easy to run. However, you may find it necessary to increase your income through expanding your passive income channels or combining them.

These tasks can be outsourced and you can eliminate them from your schedule.

This special report will discuss the best strategies and tips to create passive income streams so that you can achieve true financial freedom.

Chapter 1: Some Passive Income Strategies

There are numerous ways to earn passive income. But, all of these numerous ways require us to do one or more of the following:

Invest money

Some investments need great financial resource before they can begin to pay huge returns.

Rent out property

Some investments require you to purchase property for rental. Whether cash or credit or loans, money is required upfront.

Market our skills

You can invest your skill (s) like your knowledge as a web-designer, or programmer, or your expertise in photography, cooking, writing, teaching and so on.

Invest our time

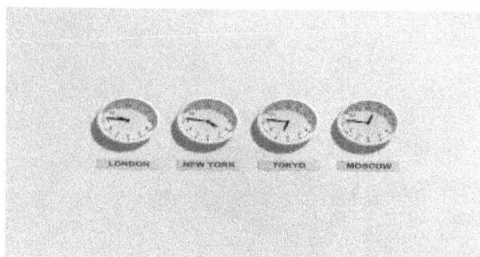

All investments need us to put in our time. Some investments need more time than others. The stock market may take more money and less time. However, creating a successful blog may take more time and less money.

Some General Investment Strategies

Below are some general investment strategies. After a brief discussion of the following strategies, I will focus in more detail on the **FOUR ONLINE BUSINESS** that I recommend.

Real Estate: There are numerous ways to create passive income in real estate. These include single-family units, duplexes, triplexes, apartment buildings, commercial buildings, industrial complexes that provide commercial warehouse storage or manufacturing facilities, self-storage facilities, mobile home parks, land lots, vacation rentals, hard money lending, fixing and flipping properties, and others.

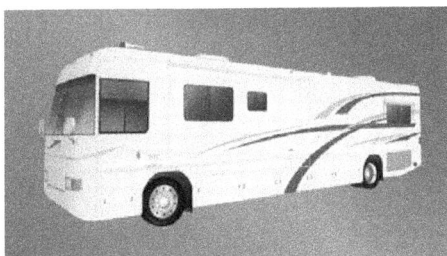

You can rent out a mobile home

Decide if you will make your **income from rental properties** or **investment portfolios.** You can invest in turnkey rental properties. These properties are ready to rent and are managed by property management companies. You can purchase houses as investment properties and rent to your ideal tenant type: families or students. Or you can buy and sell multiple properties and build equity. However, real estate investments require a great deal of time investment as you manage tenants, paperwork, and repairs. Further, this investment takes a cash flow.

Dividend Stocks:

You can invest in dividend paying stocks

This kind of investment is a relatively simple way of building long-term wealth. As your company's earnings increase, you are paid a portion of the profits in the form of dividends. You can take the cash or reinvest it by purchasing more shares. After you invest, you wait on the passive income.

Index Funds: These are mutual funds or an exchange-traded fund (ETF) linked to a particular market index. You can buy an index fund directly from a mutual fund company or a brokerage. You need to invest consistently and build up your portfolio. You can earn yearly returns of 15% or more.

Photography: For example, your expertise is photography. You have a knack for taking these really stunningly beautiful photographs. You can **license your photos to stock photography websites**.

Download photos to websites like Pixabay.com and you can earn royalties when customers use your photographs.

Internet Technology Specialist: You can **develop a mobile app.** If you have the programming skills and a relatively creative new idea, you can turn it into an app.

There are numerous opportunities in the app marketplace. Even if you have a good idea but not the expertise, you can outsource the project on FIVVER or FREELANCER or other market.

Designer: You have a knack for creativity. You can create those amusing and trendy graphics. There are countless opportunities for marketing your products for the creation of e-commerce. Designs can be placed on T-shirts, and mugs and used as logos and in countless other ways. Websites like www.Zazzle.com and www.cafepress.com can imprint your designs on all types of products.

Create an E-course: You can create an e-course about anything you are passionate about. There are millions of people out there who are interested in learning about your area of expertise.

Create an e-course

Create a Video Course: People learn in various ways, but videos can appeal to all the learning styles. There are numerous topics that you can choose from depending on your area of expertise. In addition, you can always outsource your project and have someone develop a video course for you

Publish an e-Book: There are numerous platforms for independent publishing and writers are seizing these opportunities. You do not need to wait for a publisher to release your work. You do not even need

to write the book yourself as you can outsource it on www.FIVVER.com

On www.freelancer.com and numerous other sites.

Develop an audio book. An audio book would appeal to those who primarily want to listen to a story being read and hear the nuances in the voice of the reader.

Start or buy a Blog: First, you need a specific idea and you need to identify the audience your blog will appeal to. Then you need to create the specific content or hire someone to write your content. There are many bloggers out there that earn a decent income.

You Tube Channel: Many Internet marketers are making money through their **You Tube** channel.

You do need a lot of views and this comes from being passionate about your topic area and from utilizing **AdSense** and different ways of advertising.

Sell Lesson Plans: Teachers are making passive income and sharing their knowledge by selling their lesson plans online on sites like **Teachers' Pay Teachers.**

Make a "How to" Guide: Many of us are experts in our fields. We have acquired in-depth knowledge and can create a guide to assist others who would like to acquire the specific skill.

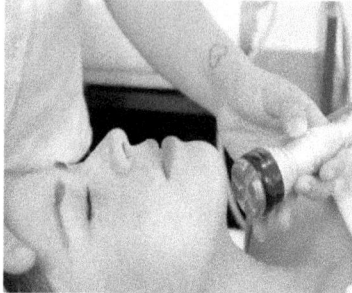

Rent Out Useful Items: You may have an extra car or truck or trailer or a bicycle or even your yard space, or a room in your house. These can be rented out and earn you passive income.

Display Ads: Display ads are similar to billboards, but they are featured on your website.

Advertisers will pay you to put these display ads on your website or blog to promote their products.

If your website generates a lot of traffic this can add up to massive passive income.

Affiliate Marketing: In affiliate marketing the owner of a product permits other marketers to sell his or her product and the seller or marketer gets a percentage from the sales made through his/her website.

The above are all excellent passive income business ventures. However, in this eBook I would recommend **FOUR** that require relatively little money invested, but a lot of time, and moreover they have the potential for delivering a good passive income.

Affiliate Marketing Passive Income

Kindle e-Book Passive Income

Online Course Passive Income

Blogging Passive Income

Chapter 2: Peer To Peer Lending

Peer to Peer (P2P) lending can aid investors in earning additional income and achieving diversification in their portfolios. P2P investing attracts a lot people who are trying to make their savings earn more money for them. In ideal situations, P2P investors can benefit from a higher return on their money, compared to what they would earn in a certificate of deposit (CD) or high-yield savings account.

To become a P2P investor you must first apply to open an account on a P2P lending platform. If you get approved, you can deposit money that will be loaned out via the platform to appropriate borrowers. You can examine loan requests and decide on the applications you'd like to accept, either disbursing the entire loan amount or a piece of it.

Via the P2P lending platform, you can track how much you've earned from principal and interest while your borrowers make payments. You can either withdraw your earnings or reinvest them.

You should be aware that there are risks involved in P2P lending, much like any other investment. There is no guarantee that your borrowers will repay as agreed. There's also the possibility that the P2P lending platform may close down. In both scenarios, you may lose a considerable amount of your investment, particularly if the loan you funded was unsecured. To shield yourself from default risk, you should diversify across hundreds of notes.

P2P lending platforms gather people intending to invest money with potential borrowers who are trying to find a loan. They act as an intermediary, by aiding in the pairing of two parties and the transfer of funds amongst them. Due to there be no conventional financial institution being a middleman, and as a result of no overheads related to banking, the borrowers and lenders may both gain from more beneficial interest rates.

P2P lending may be an alluring choice for those who are trying to enhance their investment portfolio and are prepared to bear a limited amount of risk. P2P lending may be less complicated and less volatile than investing in shares and stocks.

The P2P lending process starts with you signing up to a P2P platform and investing the amount money you intend to lend. You should then start by making lending offers to borrowers who are searching for a loan. Prior to your offer being made you should consider how long you want to offer your money for, which is typically for a fixed number of years. The longer you want to invest your money, the larger the possible returns.

After your money has been moved to your peer-to-peer account, there are usually two lending methods, a few P2P platforms will automatically make lending offers to borrowers that match your loan terms for you, while others will need you to manually do it. Even though independently overseeing each loan grants you the utmost control, it may consume more of your time. Thus, the automated lending method is less time-consuming and guarantees that your funds are always invested.

After you have been paired with one or more borrowers and the loan has been paid out, you will start to earn interest.

Given the platform you've chosen, you'll be provided with management opportunities for what you wish to do with your earnings. The best platforms will provide you with an automatic re-lending service, whereby the repayments allocated to your account are automatically disbursed for lending again, thereby optimising your returns.

There will usually be a choice which, enables you to receive a consistent income from your repayments, typically every week or month. You can also decide whether you wish to withdraw the full repayments or only the interest you have earned. This may typically be set up automatically, or with the choice to manually manage your earnings.

Numerous peer-to-peer investors tend to receive annual investment returns that exceed 10%. Normal loan rates provided by the P2P platforms range from 6% to 36%.

P2P platforms, give you more control over the specific investments compared to a majority of other investment vehicles. You can choose notes based on certain standards, such as debt-to-income ratio, loan term, credit-score range, and loan type. Thus, you are able to control the factors influencing your investments.

The best Peer-To-Peer Lending Sites for investors include Kiva, StreetShares, FundingCircle, Peerform, Lending Club, Upstart, and Prosper.

Chapter 3: How To Create Your Own Flawless Passive Income Stream?: Make Necessary Corrections Yourself

It's not easy to take a neutral look at every single aspect of a business, and more importantly when it's being run by you. But this quality can help you a lot in improving yourself and create your way to maximize the benefits. This will help you to make major corrections and update the entire strategy and make it better. You can only create a flawless system if you know how to review and monitor a strategy and make corrections by yourself. Here's how you can do this:

1 detach yourself temporarily

First, you need to detach yourself temporarily from business operation. You cannot simply start reviewing, monitoring and inspect some issues, being a part of itself. You have to work as an independent entity to get the best results. That's why you need to start working on detaching your involvement and once done; you can start reviewing and making comments from a neutral point of view and can offer effective correctional strategies.

2 take a look at the past

It's very important for everyone to take a look into the past. If you don't follow the past and learn from the mistakes, you won't be able to avoid the mistakes you did in the past. You should go through the history, find out the issues you had to face and take notes on every resolution been offered to solve the problems. This would help you to get a privileged sneak-peek into the issue, and it can help you a lot.

3 trial and error

Finally, you have to work with the most traditional approaches towards making corrections in a faulty system. Yes, you have to do a lot of trials and errors to get the right way to fix something. You have to spend time on trialing things and fixing the errors accordingly. This can only help you to make quicker and more effective corrections. You need to have your strategy to perform these on errands, and these will help you to become successful with all your efforts and other combined strategies.

Chapter 4: Why Blogging?

Blogging may not seem like the most lucrative source of passive income, especially given how flashy YouTube is in comparison, but you'd be surprised how much money a blog can produce. You know how when you Google things, all these different websites come up to give you the answer to your question? Well, all those websites are making money every time you click on one of them.

The secret to blogging is really simple. You want to provide answers for terms that people are Googling and get as many people to click on your links as possible. If you're good at this, you can be consistently ranked for terms that are very commonly searched for and always will be. We call these evergreen posts. Your goal as a blogger should be to produce this kind of evergreen content, which will continue to generate income for you far into the foreseeable future.

About Evergreen Content

So what is evergreen content? I'll give you an example and you'll very quickly be able to spot the difference. Evergreen content is **always relevant**. Here are some examples of evergreen content vs. non-evergreen content:

Evergreen Content:

- How to Make a Grilled Cheese Sandwich

- 10 Tips for Beginning Stock Market Investing

- 5 Great Exercises You Can Do at Home

- Funny Dad Jokes for Your Next Party

Non-Evergreen Content:

- The Best Bicycle of 2020

- Coca Cola Stock is Surging!

- My Iron Man 2 Review

- Why Blockbuster Will Always Survive

As you can see, the difference is, people are going to be Googling "how to make a great grilled cheese sandwich" for as far into the foreseeable future as you can imagine. Meanwhile, who cares about Iron Man 2 anymore? That's the difference between evergreen and non-evergreen content. As a rule of thumb: news & reviews are **not** evergreen and how-to guides typically **are** as long as the subject is something humans are probably going to enjoy for a long time and not just a trend like rollerblading or Pokemon GO.

Income Expectations

It is not uncommon for good bloggers to make $4,000, $6,000, even $10,000 a month, even if they don't lift a finger throughout the entire month. The way they're able to accomplish this is that they do a lot of upfront work producing the answers to these kinds of evergreen search terms across one site or multiple sites. Let me contrast how this money making strategy works against what you're mostly likely doing selling your time for money.

Mary, an experienced blogger, makes $3,000 a month. Joe, a midlevel corporate employee, makes $19/hr, which works out to about $3,000 a month. Joe puts in a hard day's work and his employer pays him $152. Mary puts in the same 8 hours of work and produces 4 posts, each of which produces $10 a month every month for the next several years. While Mary didn't make as much money **that day**, now Mary makes $3,040 a month and Joe still makes $3,000 a month. If Mary can do that every day, by the end of the month, she makes $4,200 a month from that point forward, even if she completely stops working, and Joe still has to put in his solid 8 hours a day to make his $3,000 a month.

It may seem like that's an extreme example, but it's really not. The only thing exaggerated about that is the idea that Mary is going to produce 4 posts every single day in a month. That's 120 posts a month! So, it'd probably take 2-3 months for Mary to produce that amount of content. After a year, Mary is getting more money every month without having to ever work again if she chooses not to than Joe would get if he stayed at the same company for 10 years, competing with all of his coworkers for modest 10-15% raises.

The reason blogging is an excellent source of passive income is not only way that the income compounds, just like in the above example, but also because it costs very little and mostly only requires time and expertise as an investment. Normally that expertise can only be gained as you invest more and more time, so you'll make very little to start with, but this guide will impart a tremendous amount of **my** hard-earned experience onto you so you can have a headstart in building your first asset on the way to financial freedom.

Blogging vs. YouTube

Now, a lot of people will scoff at blogging and suggest YouTube instead. Here's the problem with that. While YouTube is a fantastic way to make money, it's a lot more difficult to make money **passively** through YouTube. Although you can produce evergreen content on YouTube, the YouTube algorithm rewards new content, so if you invest your time heavily in YouTube, it's out of the frying pan and into the fryer. You're trading your day job for another day job. PewDiePie, one of the most successful YouTubers of all time, records new videos every day, and that's the norm.

Another thing is that YouTube has a lot more upfront barriers to entry. While you can start making a (small) amount of blogging very quickly after setting up your blog via AdSense ads or Affiliate Marketing, with YouTube you're not going to be able to monetize your channel **at all** until you have a significant amount of subscribers (~1,000). It also has a bigger barrier of entry in terms of cost and production value.

If you speak English, which you probably do, you can at the very least start a decent blog as long as you have a good idea of what you want to talk about and you choose something relevant that other people want to hear about. If you have a YouTube channel, you do need that idea, but the idea's not enough. You also need a camera, you need to understand video editing. Not only is it more expensive to create a video, it's more time consuming and more complex as well.

Another major difference between blogging and YouTube is what people use each platform for. Typically, when you visit Google or another search engine, which is where the majority of traffic for blogs and websites comes from, you're looking for information. If you're searching YouTube, you're typically looking for entertainment. This is a very important thing to remember. It's not a hard and fast rule, but it's typically the case. So if you're blogging, you want to provide information which is much easier than entertainment. If you're capable of creating entertaining videos, you're going to have a real edge when it comes to YouTube.

This information vs entertainment dynamic isn't just about what people are making on the channel, it's about how audience is grown in each platform. Typically, an audience for a blog is mostly first-time visitors who are looking for an answer to a specific question, whereas YouTube relies on developing a following of subscribers who repeatedly return to engage with content because they like a particular personality.

That's not to say YouTube isn't a great source of passive income, but I would recommend you start with blogging, because YouTube requires a great deal more time, energy, money and talent to turn into a viable income-generating asset.

Choosing Your Niche

So you've decided you want to get started blogging. As I mentioned above, you're going to need to have a good idea of what you want to talk about, and you want that thing to be evergreen and you want it to be relevant to other people so that they're searching for the content you're providing.

In blogging jargon, we call this choosing your niche. A niche is like a topic. It's the demographic, market, subgroup or interest group you're trying to target. Some typical niches in blogging include:

- Finance

- Cooking

- Travel

- Sports

- Parenting

- Cars

- Fashion

- Technology

- ... and many more

Basically, any common hobby or interest can be a viable niche. Anything that a lot of people love and are searching for information about, you can take advantage of. Now, it's obviously best if your niche is something **you're** interested in as well, ideally at an expert level, because it's very important that you have something meaningful to say to people in your blog posts. You can share information for beginners, valuable insight, or anything else you can think of.

The most important thing to think about when you're choosing your niche is, as I mentioned above, **your personal**

experience and expertise. If you decide to start an investing blog and you don't know anything about investing, you're not going to get very far, especially when your competitors are all providing valuable insight and expertise. More importantly, perhaps, if you're not blogging about a hobby or topic that really engages you, you're going to get burned out and you're going to give up before the money starts coming in.

On average, it'll take you between 6 months and a year of regular blogging to be making your first $1000 a month. There's a bit of exponential growth there (going from $1000/mo to $2000/mo is a lot easier than going from $0/mo to $1000/mo), so once you reach that point you're probably going to be in really good shape. 6 months to a year or probably an average of about 400 total posts. If you don't know or like investing, are you going to be able to make 400 total posts or keep up with it for a year? That's a long time to fake interest in a topic.

However, if you just absolutely love traveling and you travel all the time even if you're not being paid for it, all you need to do is commit to doing a travel diary for each trip, maybe a top 10 places to visit post, a few other types of posts you figure out over time get great traffic and you'll reach 400 posts over a year without any burnout whatsoever. In fact, you'll probably really enjoy it.

Competition & Ad Rates

Now that we've made sure you're blogging about something you know and love, it's time to tell you a little bit more about the business side of things, because it's important to be aware of that aspect as well. Ultimately, it all boils down to writing great content, but you're going to want to be aware of two business related realities when you're deciding on your niche: competition and ad rates.

Ad Rates

Let's talk about ad rates first. Basically, when you're advertising on your website, some niches get much better rates from advertisers when they sell their ad space. For example, Finance and Tech products tend to do really well. Medicine also tends to give really good payouts. We call these ad rates RPMs or "Revenue per Mille". Essentially, RPM is the amount of money you make per 1,000 views.

So, if you're running a Finance blog, it's not unheard of to see $30-$40 RPM rates at quality ad management companies, or even $15-18 RPMs on entry level ad services like AdSense. This means your fledgling Finance blog with 30,000 views a month could be making $540 a month, while your Needlepoint Enthusiast blog with the exact same number of views only pulls in a paltry $60.

You should consider this, but don't think about it **too much** because, like I said, you're not going to succeed with a Finance blog if you don't know anything about Finance (your posts will fail) or you have no passion for that topic (you'll burn out and quit). Still, if you're passionate and knowledgeable about more than one area, you may want to consider which one will make you more money.

How do you know? Well, it's not difficult to find testimonials online, but they're mostly anecdotal. The general rule of thumb is that expensive but highly specialized services tend to offer the best rates. For example, Finance, Marketing,

Legal, Medical, etc. Niches that tend to **underperform** are ones that advertise cheap but also highly specialized services. The needlepoint example above is pretty good. Surfing would be another example.

Most people want to write about something that excites them, which is often some form of entertainment. Entertainment is medium-low in terms of RPMs. Parenting is medium-high. Cars are medium-high. If you really think about it hard enough, it tends to be exactly what you'd expect. If you're a huge movie buff, how much do you spend on that interest annually vs. someone who's really into cars? In that way, you can see how a car blog will probably get higher RPMs than a movie blog.

This is not only because of the interest itself, but also because of product relevance. Advertisers try to fill your ad space with content relevant to your audience. When there isn't enough ad inventory that's directly related to your topic, they'll broaden out their search and fill your ad space to other products it thinks the demographic that reads your blog may like, reducing relevance and thus reducing interest and thus reducing your ad revenue.

To continue the cars vs. movies contrast, a car blog may be able to advertise all sorts of car services, car parts, new cars, etc. All pricey services with fantastic relevance to the blog content. On the movie blog, however, they'll advertise a few new movies that come out each month, maybe a new service like MoviePass, a different movie blog (ouch), but it won't be enough to fill your ad inventory so they'll quickly default to filler ads like grocery stores, car insurance, etc., which your audience will likely ignore. That's not to say a movie blog is a **bad idea**, though. Your interest and knowledge is the most important thing. A successful movie blog getting 500,000 visitors a month and $8 RPMs is going to make a lot more money than a terrible car blog with 40,000 visitors a month and $20 RPMs.

I mean, ultimately you're doing this for lifestyle, right? What's the point in quitting the job you hate to spend all your time for a year working on a blog you hate? My biggest blog, speaking personally, is in a medium-low RPM niche and it's one of the top performing blogs out there right now purely because of the sheer volume of traffic it gets. So be aware of those RPMs, maybe pick the highest RPM category you're passionate about, but don't just pick a high RPM category because of the money. You will fail, I promise.

COMPETITION

Next, let's discuss the other business reality you need to consider when choosing your niche, which is competition. The fact of the matter is most well-known niches already have a ton of active blogs in their space. That means competition.

Keep in mind you're trying to make your blog posts show up on Google when people are searching for specific questions. Go ahead and visit Google right now and search for a question. See how there are tons of different options there? And what do you, as a searcher do? You click on the first or second one, usually, right? And then only if that didn't answer your question do you move onto the rest. You very, very rarely go to page 2 or more unless you're looking for something that's really hard to find.

That's where the competition comes into play. You want to be the first or second link on Google. We call this a search engine rank placement or SERP. That means your content either needs to be better than what currently ranks #1, or you need to be answering questions no one else is providing a satisfying answer for.

Knocking other sites from #1 so you can occupy the slot is a bit more difficult and requires leveraging something called Domain Authority, as well as a pretty good understanding of SEO (search engine optimization) and Schema (a bit of a more advanced topic in terms of SEO), all of which you most likely don't have a good command over as a brand new blogger, although you can do it from time to time just purely by delivering better content, and you should certainly try.

This means you typically want to target subcategories of major niches that still get great interest and people are still searching for, but don't have quite as much competition. For instance, maybe you don't want to cover cars, maybe you want to cover collectible classic cars. Maybe you shouldn't do movies maybe you should do sci-fi movies. Then, over time, you can begin to outrank the big guys on your own topic.

This goes into what I mentioned earlier about domain authority. Let me give you an example. You're doing your collectible classic cars blog. Someone is searching for the coolest cars from 1969. They see at rank #1 there's a list of 1969 cars from "EverythingCars.com" and then at rank #2 they see "Top 10 Most Amazing Cars from the Late 60s" from "CollectibleClassicCars.com". What will they click? What would you click? The specialized one, right? Over time, Google picks up on things like that, you rank higher in your niche and you start to develop what website ranking companies refer to as Domain Authority, which makes it easier for you to rank over the long run.

So yeah, Finance is a great niche, right? But go Google Finance and you'll quickly learn the MotleyFool, NerdWallet, etc are all extremely dominant in the Finance niche. It would be hard to outrank them without sufficient domain authority. So it's often best to start with a sub-category of a major existing niche **or** a niche that doesn't have as much competition to begin with (for example: surfing).

Now that you've figured out your niche, or what you're going to be writing about, the next thing you need to do is get started, and the first thing you need to do to get started is get a domain name and some quality webhosting.

Chapter 5: Make Money while You Sleep. Why the Hell not?

What does it sound like to make money every day while you have a siesta? Would you be interested in that?

I am 100% certain that everyone reading this will find the answer to their question "yes". Possibly you'll even get smarter than me and ask, "Who wouldn't?"

This is not realistic for most people. Money doesn't fall out of trees. The ones that seem to do so are likely to con you into spending your money in the hope that you'll make more.

While you may not be able make it big, you can still earn a decent income regardless of how hard you work. This quick guide will help you stop "shopping your time for money" or "trading your time for dollars."

This is where passive income income comes in to play. We will show you how to create business models that can sustain themselves with minimal effort.

Yes. Yes, you read that right. It is possible to create an automated system for selling ads or recommending products. You can make money all the time!

You only need to do some initial work. Then, you can relax and watch the money roll into your bank account.

It's simple, just think about it. You won't trade your time for money with the methods that we will teach you. This means you will go to bed feeling a lot better the next day. While I don't claim that you can become a millionaire overnight but it will be possible to pay more bills without spending a lot of money. You'll also be able to travel and earn while you enjoy a relaxing vacation in Thailand or Europe. You can simply drop everything you are doing and go to your child or family member's request for mandatory bonding.

These passive income methods can be automated, meaning that they require little to no input from you. This means you can keep repeating the same strategies over and again to increase your earnings. This is called'scaling. You adapt new methods or modify existing ones to make more money. With enough effort, you could eventually be making huge amounts of money by having multiple income streams that all work at once.

Does it sound too good to be true

Yes. It's also true.

Chapter 6: Top 20 Best Future Business Ideas For 2020-2030

Continuing from where the last chapter ended...

Asteroid Mining

Do you know that precious material like silver, gold, diamonds, and platinum are found all over space? Space travel is still developing and is expected to become even more advanced. One of the first issues that corporations will address will have to do with mining asteroid for precious minerals like diamond and gold.

This is a serious and major undertaking that may not even be feasible until 2030. However, it is worth investing in, and many big companies are presently and extremely focused on this.

Research has shown that even a tiny section of space could be worth more than double the Earth's entire wealth. This means that the first set of individuals who manage to get a spacecraft to a resource-loaded asteroid could quickly become the world's wealthiest people.

Investing in asteroid mining could be capital-intensive as you may need to create robots and drones that will aid in drilling as well as mining asteroids. Whichever way you see it, this is an industry with a lot of incredible potentials and, of course, for people who are daring enough to try the impossible.

eCommerce

The world has virtually moved online, changing almost everything from the way things are purchased to delivery at your doorstep. Businesses that are not taking a leaf from the eCommerce industry run the risk of getting left behind.

This year alone, it has an estimated that consumers in the United States will spend more than $709 billion on eCommerce, representing a growth rate of 18 percent. This is slated to hit up to $4.9 trillion by 2021.

One thing is sure: eCommerce is the retail market tomorrow. And what makes eCommerce unique is that you do not even have to own or make the products you sell. All that you need to do is to utilize another aspect of eCommerce known as Dropshipping.

You can also choose to be an affiliate, a system of selling products which is explained later on. The truth is that the financial advantages of running an eCommerce business are staggering. Take a look at the following eCommerce highlights:

Higher ROIs

Elevated business reach

Easy to track

More search engine traffic

Logistically solid

Flexible, scalable, and profitable

Automated product delivery systems

There is no better period to get online than now because, by 2030, the majority of shopping will be conducted online, i.e., digitally. Consumers will only use brick and mortar establishments as an experience. And such businesses will need to make considerable changes such as price reductions and specialization if they hope to stay in the game extensively.

Wallet Payment Solution

Wallet payment solutions have been somewhat slow to catch on in the U.S.A. Nevertheless, it is a market that is on its way to becoming a national corporation.

Wallet payment has to do with monetary transactions made with a virtual or digital wallet via a software program. It securely stores people's payment details and ensures purchases are super-easy.

This money-making concept is somewhat unknown in the United States because most people living in the country possess credit and debit cards, which are convenient, simple, and trusted means of payment.

Nevertheless, wallet payment solutions are taking some countries – such as China and India – by storm. Therefore, it is merely a question of time before the trend will take hold in the U.S. as well as other parts of the globe. It is currently projected to be worth an estimated and whopping $130 billion by the end of 2020.

This market has some established and hefty competition like Masterpass, ApplePay, and Chase Pay. However, it is just proof that there is a lot of money to be made in this industry since these brands are players there.

You can secure profitability in this industry that will soon change the entire trajectory of the world's future within a short time.

Virtual Interior Design Consulting

Interior design is all about placement and visuals, as well as the ability to transform a space into a comfortable and scenic sanctuary for clients.

The advent and rise of technology have made it possible for enthusiasts to launch an interior design business and run it from the sanctuary of their homes with nothing but a laptop, camera gear, tablet, software, and social media.

You will see the exterior and interior of a client's office space or property via the lens of your camera. Then, the next thing that you should do is to create stunning mockups for your clients, send them over, and consult regarding the next step to take.

As you well know, the marketing of your new remote interior design and consulting business will depend significantly on social media, your official website as well as getting in touch with your current connections within your network while working hard to create new ones.

Affiliate Marketing

Affiliate Marketing involves the promotion of someone else's products – using any means at your disposal – that you love or have tried and tested. And if someone purchases that product based on your promotion efforts and testimonials, you will receive a commission.

This is an online marketing model that you can leverage without doing the tough job of creating the product, handling customer complaints or support, and so on.

This is a business model that works incredibly well that up to 81 percent of businesses are currently taking advantage of this model in one way or the other. And if you set things up the right way, you can be making money passively or in your sleep for many years to come as long as your niche site remains live on the web.

IT Service and Support

The face of the corporate world will eventually be digital since more and more businesses, and individuals will continue to rely even more heavily on the internet as well as social media platforms. There will be a proliferation of software and hardware to contend favorably with this immense growth.

These vital tools will ultimately generate an influx in demand for both IT service and support enterprises. The projected growth rate for IT services is up to 22 percent in 2020 alone. Software development and other facets are seeing upwards of 32 percent growth rate, making it one of the best future business ideas to explore today.

Many business and individuals from around the world will need help with setup and maintenance and troubleshooting issues. This is because the most of the population in the United States is astonishingly clueless when it comes to tech stuff.

Remarkable advancements in technology around Cloud computing, Blockchain, AI, and even elevated automation will leave some of the most tech-savvy individuals and organizations seeking professional assistance. This is where you will come in as the messiah, especially if you love tech stuff or prefer to be called a tech nerd.

The options within the IT service and support niche are numerous, and this includes:

IT Managers

Database Admins

Product Manager

Software Inventory

Blockchain Engineer

Cloud Architect

DevOps Designer

Artificial Intelligence Engineer of AI Engineer

This is just a small section of an extensive list that you can explore to your satisfaction.

VR Live Events

Is there an annual conference that you can't make or want to enjoy your favorite band while still on tour? Do you even know that you can get a ticket for those events and experience them as if you were there in the flesh from your study or living room?

This is made possible thanks to VR, which helps individuals worldwide to readily access live events, helping the hosts generate mouth-watering and untold revenue.

At present, the revenue for virtual events is up to $78 billion, and projections currently suggest that this number will significantly grow to a breathtaking $774 billion by 2030.

Believe it or not, everything from conferences and exhibitions to music concerts is headed in the direction of virtual implementation. This implies that there won't be a limit to the sale of tickets based on the availability of space as it will now be possible to sell hundreds of millions of tickets to in-person and virtual spectators.

The adoption of VR for the modern world was not expected to take off as it did, but the scourge of the pandemic saw to it. The industry has been predicted to witness an unbelievable CAGR of 33.47 percent, which speaks volumes about its profitability for businesses in the space.

As it stands, the projected growth rate will even be much higher than this.

Virtual Event Planning Platform

Event planning has now taken on a new look and is presently leaning even more on online and virtual affairs.

Video streaming services have successfully eliminated geographical constraints, thereby allowing event planners to host exceptional virtual events to remote audiences. Embracing this virtual event to maintain cash flow and profitability is the best way for event planners to stay in business in these modern times.

To execute stellar events online, the following crucial fundamentals must be in place:

Pick your platform

Understand the needs as well as the expectations of your audience

Develop or create your format and how you intend to make your event unique

Determine the venue, day, and time

Choose an MC or host that can captivate your audience and is highly entertaining.

Always keep it simple, short, and to the point.

Event planners provide both a service and an experience. This is a business model that will continue to generate substantial profits with some creativity and the right infrastructure, as well as the willingness to shift to online solutions.

Tele and Video Conferencing

The pandemic has touched all aspects of the economy, especially face-to-face interactions and regular office work. It has resulted in the significant adoption of teleconferencing and video conferencing, and businesses like Zoom has climbed up Forbes' list, thanks to massive signups and subscriptions from multi-national organizations. The virtual meetings hosted by Zoom over the past few months cannot be quantified.

This can only mean one thing: video conferencing and teleconferencing are the new norms on how to conduct business transactions. From business communication and networking, teleconferencing provides individuals and associates worldwide the opportunity and ability to maintain highly productive or effective communication even amid the global pandemic.

The education industry has also taken a hit and has adopted teleconferencing and video conferencing as the best way to overcome the throes of COVID-19.

What if you had foreseen this circumstance and bought shares or even owned at least one of these teleconferencing and video conferencing conglomerates? That would have been cool, isn't it? Well, it is not too late because this business venture still has a futuristic appeal.

According to a well-researched publication, teleconferencing and video conferencing have been projected to see a growth rate of approximately 9.8 percent from 2020-2026. And it will purportedly reach a market value of more than $6 billion in the United States of America alone. This is too huge a pie to pass up, especially if you want to get in on the action in this growing industry that is reaching record highs and breaking barriers left, right, and center.

Teleconferencing, as well as video conferencing, efficiently delivers alternate options in order to maintain productivity, efficiency, and personalization.

eSports

eSports offer a gamer's paradise with the competitive edge of live competitions. Organized tournaments in several sports –

via video games – have started taking on a digital presence, as well as a lot of people around the world are taking notice.

And with the way the popularity of eSports is growing, it is presently estimated that viewership will see a CAGR of 9 percent from 2020-2023, and will purportedly fetch revenues that is more than 4646 million by the end of that stipulated time frame.

Game enthusiasts love the social component of eSports, and you will agree that we are a highly competitive bunch in any field. Live streaming, and social media platforms, are generally the driving forces behind the remarkable growth of this industry with no sign of slowing down.

And you can take a slice of this cake by jumping in on the action today. You can launch an eSports platform of your own as long as you are ready to adhere to the following recommendations:

Choose your ideal target market and geographical area.

Hone down the niche; pick one popular sport that you love and get after it.

Organize your team and don't forget to include branding

Put your infrastructure in place with the appropriate hardware. This should include a user-friendly eSports website.

Secure sponsorships in order to fund this endeavor to enable you to compete at an elevated position.

Remember to pick a location and aggressively promote your team.

Fans, as well as additional recruitment options, is a must.

There is no doubt that eSports is presently revolutionizing virtual, competitive gaming and is considered one of the best future business ideas to adopt for 2020-2030. You can conduct in-depth research to ascertain what it takes to be incredibly successful in this 21st-century business.

In the next two chapters, we will be taking a look at Facebook Marketing and YouTube Marketing. Implementing these marketing strategies incredibly well has the potential of generating passive income for you.

Chapter 7: Affiliate Marketing

By offering the proportion of the margin of your product or service to a large number of affiliates, you can dramatically boost sales albeit at a lower overall margin rate. By sharing the profits of a sale with other websites, it is possible for webmasters to generate higher sales volumes. By devising an attractive affiliate scheme and promoting and implementing that scheme in a professional manner, it is possible to generate thousands of website visitors using an affiliate of channel online. Search engines become less relevant if affiliates are sending your website the bulk of its traffic. Amazon.com is one of the pioneers of this business model selling million of books via ten's of thousand's of Amazon affiliates. Today, affiliate marketing is a very well established method of selling online. The main advantage of affiliate marketing is high sales volume with nominal sales effort at an extremely low cost. The main disadvantage is much lower margins, (as affiliates need paying commission to remain motivated).

What is an Affiliate Program?

An affiliate program is a contractual arrangement between the owner of a product or service (the Merchant) and a separate 'Affiliate' organisation, to pay a commission, in exchange for promotion of its goods and services. Typically, this entails an affiliate website adding advertisements (in the form of banners, buttons links and other textual material) promoting the Merchants offering. There are literally thousands of different affiliate programs in existence on the Internet today. It is usually the responsibility of the affiliate to redirect visitors to their website to the merchant's website. At that point any customer service issues (such as ordering a product, dealing with customers on telephone delivering issues) are dealt with by the Merchant.

Affiliate schemes are normally automated and structured. Affiliates must pre-agree to abide by the merchant's terms and conditions when signing up before entitled to promote anything. For instance, Merchants make it a condition that affiliates do not alter the Merchant sales copy to avoid any potential accidental or deliberate misrepresentation (and ultimately customer dissatisfaction). Affiliates usually have a unique tracking ID associated to their registration or website. By adding this html code to their site, Merchants can track where each individual sale came from. The tracking html is usually combined with a cookie or CGI script to allow the Merchants Affiliate Tracking system to collate a database of visitors and sales. It is normal that affiliates get paid one month in arrears and have an access to a monthly report outlining leads, sales and conversions. Affiliates are primarily motivated by money and so they are usually very interested in knowing the conversion rate of the Merchant.

Merchants benefit hugely from an affiliate marketing model as there is a virtual unlimited supply of keen entrepreneurs seeking out business opportunities to make money (in exchange for promoting an online business idea). Most affiliate schemes operate in a commission scheme based on payments monthly in arrears, payable from the merchant to the affiliate of either via PayPal or an alternative independent escrow service, or check in the post. Some merchants exclude or reject applications from prospective affiliates who do not meet their guidelines for type of website, physical location or regulatory approvals (particularly in Financial Services). The main benefit of an electronic affiliate business model is that it is completely scalable - it is possible to recruit an unlimited number of affiliates to promote your product and the cost of doing so can be negligible.

Types of Commission Schemes

There are various types of affiliate models in use today. Historically, affiliate models existed based on banner advertising which were rewarded on a per impression basis. However, click through ratios were extremely poor and banner exchange schemes gave the sector a bad name. In addition, fraud impacted confidence in this method of marketing. The last nail in the coffin for banner advertising was that 'in your face' flashy moving images also tended to annoy users. Today, textual ads are the primary form of affiliate marketing. These are highly customised to the users needs using contextual advertising (based on the user's individual search profile and IP geographic location) are the preferred means of advertisers to reach their target markets.

• Pay per sale

The merchant pays the affiliate an agreed sum of money each time a user visits the affiliate's website, clicking through's to the merchant website, and buys something. Most merchants affiliate programs tend to have a fixed commission schemes on a pay per sale basis. This could mean either a commission value for sale or a commission based on a percentage of the sale. These tend to have certain restrictions or caveats such as a minimum order a sale value, whether the client is a new business customer or existing customer. In addition, there may be bonuses based on volume of sales over a given period - all these types factors are used as carrots and sticks to motivate affiliates to behave in a certain way.

•Pay-per-click

This affiliate commission scheme is based on the number of unique visitor clicks from an affiliate website through to the merchant's website. Unique clicks are identified using IP tracking to prevent click fraud. The user clicks on a text link with an embedded affiliate code or perhaps clicks on a search result or advert. The commission per click is obviously a lot lower than on a pay per sale basis. The affiliate benefits from of an instant and reliable source of commission. If the number of click thorough's from an affiliate's site is high and conversion rates of the merchant low, a pay per click model is ideal to maximise commission.

•Pay per lead

A pay per lead of commission based model is typically used by merchants in situations where the product or service cannot be easily downloaded or purchased using your credit card, or where the sale requires human call-back and has a long sales cycle. For instance, where the merchant is a mortgage broker and requires the user to fill in a call back form with their contact details on. Each completed contact form would count as a 'lead' and will be paid to the affiliates on a qualified 'per lead' basis.

•Two Tier Affiliate Schemes

A two tier affiliate scheme is a multi tiered program where affiliates in the first level of can also earn commission from the sale was generated from affiliates that they are recruit who sit in the second level or 'tier'. Typically the first tier would earn 10% commission on sales it indirectly generates from Merchant sales. In addition, the affiliate may earn a much smaller percentage e.g. 2% from sales from 2nd tier affiliates they recruited to the Merchant. A two tier scheme is aimed to motivate affiliates to recruit like minded people to also become affiliates.

It requires additional sales copy marketing material and a good quality affiliate manager software tool. This tool links affiliates together and details of any sales, in order to calculate potentially vast commission sums. Key to success is a higher margin product, where margin can be allocated two separate levels to the point where affiliate's remain motivated and enthusiastic.

•Affiliate Networks

An affiliate network website is an independently run collection of affiliate schemes which allow members of the network to join either one, some or all of the affiliate schemes registered with the affiliate network. It is a club making recruit of affiliates a straight forward process. This is ideal for portal websites where a range of different topics and schemes that can be advertised across a large number of different pages. Affiliate networks charge the Merchant to be part of the network and may even take a large slice of affiliates commission.

In exchange, the affiliate network provides the merchant with an instant access to hundreds or even thousands of potential affiliates who have already joined the network in the past. In addition, it provides a central management console for affiliate's to track sales and leads. It is quite simply a middleman for a large and complex number of affiliate schemes all promoting themselves alongside their competitors. An example of an affiliate network is Commission Junction.

•Critical success factors

There are usually a range of factors that are critical to the success of your affiliate Marketing strategy:

High Commissions - affiliates marketing efforts are directly proportional to the commission they receive (relative to your competitors affiliate commission levels). A successful affiliate business model relies on a sensible amount of available margin to be divided between the website owner and its affiliate on each sale.

•Offer a Differentiated or Unique Product or Service

prospective affiliates will be attracted to have something a bit different with professional online marketing literature. If your web site is very similar to dozens of other websites, all promoting their own affiliate scheme, why should a prospective affiliate sign up to your affiliate scheme as opposed to your competitors? Therefore, you must really try and sell to the prospective affiliate (via your website affiliate signup page), in order to recruit them as an affiliate. It is critical to summarise your unique selling points so they can clearly see there is an opportunity to make money together.

•Quality Feedback & Reporting

constant reassurance through online reporting and real time statistics help motivate affiliates. The more management information you can provide to an affiliate, the more confidence they will have in your ability have to close the sale. As an affiliate, it is a real confidence boost to see an email confirmation every time a lead is generated or sale made that has come from the affiliate's website. Consequently, the more motivated they will be to send additional leads in the future.

•Great Merchant Customer Service

By providing professional and service to your prospects, your sales conversion ratio obviously improves. Prospective affiliate's will be looking for affiliate schemes that provide good quality conversion ratios and have a good market reputation. Affiliates need to know that that every single visitor they send to your site has the greatest possible chance of making the money vie you're selling effort. There is nothing more de-motivating for an affiliate than a lead that does not get followed up quickly enough or is accidentally deleted or ignored by the merchant.

•Merchant Affiliate Recruitment Efforts

Patience/ time to recruit the desired number of motivated affiliates is very important.. . Ask yourself basic questions... if it takes 6 months to recruit 100 affiliates who generate 200 sales equivalent to £100,000 profit in that time, could you have generated more than 200 sales in that time (and at what profit) if you had concentrated on direct selling only.

•Affiliate Management & Tracking Systems

As the merchant you must have a thorough understanding of online affiliate tracking software and services to ensure affiliates are paid on time, sales are allocated fairly and automated new affiliate recruitment can be initiated. If you have no systems in place there are many commercial affiliate services available or software packages to provide an end to end service to manage and track affiliate's leads and sales. This is equally important for accounting purposes as the bigger your affiliate program becomes, the more important it is to justify outgoing costs (affiliate commission payments).

Things You Didn't Know About Affiliate Marketing

Most people have heard of affiliate marketing, even if they haven't actually started doing it. Affiliate marketing is basically referring people to various products and services around the internet. For each sale you generate through your affiliate link, you earn a commission. The size of the commission depends on the products themselves, who is selling them and the percentage offered by the seller to the affiliate.

But what is actually involved in affiliate marketing? What do affiliates do on a daily basis? How do they earn money and how do they learn what to do?

•An Example Of A Successful Website

There's several ways of marketing products and services online. Many affiliates create a blog first and sell products and services through their blog. Martin Lewis has a very successful website called moneysavingexpert.com. This is also an affiliate website. By creating content and helping people decide which service to use: which credit card offers to choose, the best interest rate etc. moneysavingexpert.com makes money by sending website visitors to various offers. If a sale is made through this website, the link this credited to it and a commission is made. By creating content, offering value and helping people make sensible choices, the website has built a reputation and become more prevalent over time. Google ranks the site highly in the search engines and thousands of people use it to make purchasing decisions every day.

•How Can I Get Started As An Affiliate?

Affiliate marketing is huge. There are thousands of people already making their main source of income from the internet. To get started as an affiliate you need to learn some basic strategies and build various methods of generating traffic from the internet to those offers. A lot of affiliates start with a simple blog. Many travelers 'blog' about their travels. If you don't have a passion or interest to blog about, you can start by following an online course which will help. See my bio for more info on this.

•How Long Does It Take To Make A Living?

Some people go into affiliate marketing with the intention of creating a second income. Some people want to make big money. Depending on how much time you can dedicate to your affiliate business, and how dedicated you are to it, is a big factor in determining your results. Results vary from person to person. With a large advertising budget and the right business model, some affiliates have replaced their living in 6-12 months. For others it can take years before it replaces their existing income. Depending on your approach, advertising budget, and business model, it can take between 3 months and several years to build it to a point where it can replace an existing income.

• Can Anyone Do It?

One of the great things about affiliate marketing is that the technology is now available to allow anyone to build their own online business. As long as you are prepared to learn and implement that knowledge, anyone who can operate an email, can use online platforms and tools to build their own online business. The main thing you need is the desire to learn. Affiliate marketing isn't for everyone though. It does take a lot of hard work and it can take years before you are rewarded financially.

•What Are The Pitfalls Of An Affiliate Business?

You need to dedicate some time to your affiliate business for it to work for the long term. Some people go into affiliate marketing thinking it is some magic pill which will pay them instantly in cash. Much like a job you can't expect to get out more than you put in. Affiliate marketing is performance related. This means you don't get paid unless you can successfully sell products and services online. If you don't know what you are doing it can take years to do this. You can't be a dabbler and expect to earn the big money. The big earnings are created over years of hard work. Don't expect to achieve this with only a small amount of input.

•What Are The Best Things About Affiliate Marketing?

Affiliate marketing offers an incredible amount of flexibility and freedom. You can work an affiliate business from anywhere in the world providing you have a laptop and an internet connection. You can choose your own hours and build it up around existing work. Many people come into affiliate marketing because it offers this kind of flexibility. They can choose their priorities in life: spend more time with family, choose your working hours, travel and work abroad. No more commuting to work or working long hours for a boss you don't like.

Affiliate marketing also offers incredible scalability. A business which is local is always limited to the people who can travel to that business. An online business can be global. Using digital products in conjunction with a global reach, you can scale using tools and software to reach thousands of people through digital technology. By using automation much of the work involved with an online business can be pre-built. By building automation into the business model, you can focus your activities on reaching a larger audience through content creation and paid advertising.

•Why Am I Struggling With My Affiliate Business?

A lot of people struggle with their affiliate businesses.This can be for a number of reasons. Firstly building up an affiliate business takes time. You need to dedicate a lot of time to an affiliate business in the first place. Only when you reach a 'tipping point' do you really start to see your progress. Many affiliates simply don't realise how much work is involved. They underestimate how much time they need to dedicate to their online business to make it work.

Paid advertising can allow you to grow your affiliate business quickly. But it costs money and you need the right products too. You can't advertise small value items with paid advertising. You won't generate enough profit to cover your advertising costs. You need a range of products and an email list to advertise through.

Content marketing takes much longer to work, depending on your chosen area of business. If you find an untapped niche to market your blog in, you can make some fast progress. However, with a competitive niche you will struggle to get noticed above all the other content which you will have to compete with. There's several reasons why you might struggle. The main one is lack of knowledge. Get the right education first and your affiliate business will move much faster.

•What's The Best Affiliate Model To Use?

There are many different affiliate models, all offering something different to suit the individual. Some affiliates target search traffic and aim to get their content found on Google. Some create their own products and sell them directly to customers. However, having a range of products which you can sell over and over to existing customers is a great model for long term success. Selling a single item online is limited. It means you can only make one commission from each sale.

By choosing membership products to promote which also offer back end sales and a built in sales team, you can benefit from monthly commissions and up-sell commissions for the lifetime of any given customer. Selling membership products is definitely a game changer when it come to affiliate marketing because you make an income from each customer, rather than a single commission. But a good model to choose is one in which you have a passion for and can keep doing for the long term. Choosing products which you have no interest in is a short sighted plan. Think about what you would like to do online to generate an income. If you choose to go with your passion, your business will last much longer, and be more successful.

•Can I Just Sell My Own Products?

Many affiliates create their own products to sell online. However, when you are starting out it is a good idea to learn the basics of marketing first. That way you can start earning more quickly from your affiliate business. I spent a long time creating my own products when I first discovered affiliate marketing. But I didn't sell anything because of a couple of reasons. Firstly I didn't research whether my products would have a big enough demand. Secondly I didn't know how to market them. By joining a program which teaches you how to market products first, you can start making money more quickly.

Don't waste time creating products if you don't know how to sell them. Marketing is a much more important skill for making money online. Once you know this skill, you can then apply it later when marketing your own products and services. Also your own products will be limited in range. By using an existing product range, you can benefit from products which are already selling. You can choose a program which offers high ticket commission, monthly memberships, back end sales and a built in sales team. Building your own products which offers all of these things not a possibility for most people when starting out.

•What's The Point Of Affiliate Marketing?

Some people struggle with the concept of affiliate marketing.They think it sounds too 'salesy'. When I understood affiliate marketing I immediately found it appealing simply because I needed a flexible way to work around my contract work. I had to drop what I was doing at a moments notice if the phone went. This meant other jobs were awkward to juggle around. No-one wants to employ a 'flaky' employee. I wanted to work from my laptop and affiliate marketing gave me that opportunity. For many people this is the reason why they choose affiliate marketing.

They can earn an income from their laptop, choose their working hours and not have a boss or place of employment. You don't have to sell directly to anyone or even talk to a customer. There is no stock to hold. Added to this, the scalability of affiliate marketing which lets you scale up to a global audience and deliver products on autopilot, makes it the best flexible business of the future.

How to Make Money While You Sleep With Affiliate Marketing

Affiliate marketing is about making money. Gobs of money. Money for doing nothing.

At least that's what a quick Google search would have you believe, but as usual, the truth is a little more complex than that.

Yes, you can make money through affiliate marketing. Good money. And, yes, you can even make money while you sleep.

Affiliate marketing is a simple 3-step process:

• You recommend a product or service to your followers.

• Your followers purchase the product or service using your affiliate link.

• You get paid a commission for the sales made using your affiliate link.

Getting Started With Affiliate Marketing

Now you know the basic definition of affiliate marketing and how the process works, so let's talk about how to get started. Many would-be affiliate marketers don't take the time to plan and instead sign up for every affiliate marketing network or affiliate marketing program they can find.

They end up overwhelmed and overloaded.

Take your time and work through these 7 steps if you want to set yourself up for success. Complete the first 4 steps before you even consider promoting a single product.

•Build a Website

Once you've found a profitable niche that you're excited about, you're ready to build a website and blog. WPBeginner has a great guide to help you choose the best blogging platform that will definitely make this process a lot easier.

The primary focus of your site is going to be your blog, but there are several pages that you should consider including (and some that are a flat-out MUST for affiliate marketers):

•About: Make it personable and let people get to know you a little.

•Contact: This should include all contact information that you want to share with your readers, advertisers, or potential partners.

•Disclaimer: If your site is monetized, this is where you share the how of it.

•Privacy Policy: Let users know if you collect any information about them and how that information is used.

•Terms of Service: This is a legal page limiting your liability in the event of misuse of information or services provided on your site. It also details user responsibilities regarding copyrights and trademarks.

•Custom 404 Page: A custom 404 page goes a long way toward improving the user experience.

•Advertise: If you plan on selling on-site ads, include a page for advertisers with information about available spots, monthly views, audience demographics, and a contact form.

It's important to make sure that your policies are clear and upfront to avoid confusion and to build trust with your audience.

•Create Quality Content

Now that the framework of your page is ready to go, you need to create content. Some affiliate networks and affiliate programs require you to already have established content, site traffic, and monthly views at a certain level before they'll accept you as an affiliate, so be sure to read the eligibility requirements for the specific networks and programs you're considering before you apply.

This doesn't mean that you have to create 100 blog posts before you can even think about becoming an affiliate marketer, but you should have at least 5 strong posts already on your site with more scheduled.

•Grow Your Email List

Yes, email is still the #1 communication channel for marketing. And, it still carries a completely wild $38 return for every $1 spent. What does this mean to you? That it's 3800% worth it to invest some time and money into growing your email list.

One of the easiest ways to grow your email list is by adding a popup to your site:

•Choose Affiliate Products to Promote

If you've done the work to choose a niche, choosing affiliate products to promote should be easy! Choose products that fit your niche and relate to your content.

Where do you get ideas for products to promote? Anywhere, really:

•Promote Products you Already Use

What do you already use and love? There's probably an affiliate program for that. Make a list of all of the products and services that you use and hit up Google to find their affiliate programs. Then, write reviews and plug in the affiliate links.

Whatever you love to use, there's a good chance an affiliate program exists for it.

•Promote Products That Fill a Need

Listen to the people who are interested in your niche. What problems are they facing? Are there gaps in the solutions that are already available? Find products that can help and try them out. If the products are good, become an affiliate and recommend them. Your audience wants solutions. If they work, they'll be willing to pay for them.

•Promote Products Your Audience Wants to Know About

Ask your audience what they're interested in and try it. If it's a good product, recommend it. If it isn't, tell them. At best, you'll get sales. At worst, you'll gain more trust from your audience. Which basically means there's no "worst" here.

•Promote Products From Others in Your Niche

Pay attention to other affiliate marketers in your niche. What are they talking about and promoting? What ads are they using? Check out Instagram, Twitter, Pinterest, and Facebook to take a look at #affiliate and #ad to see what other affiliates are promoting.

•Join an Affiliate Marketing Network

Affiliate marketing networks are essentially online marketplaces where retailers list their products and affiliates can find products to sell. The marketing network acts as a middleman. As the affiliate, you should never have to pay to sign up for an affiliate marketing network.

Here are a few of the more popular affiliate networks out there, but there are so many more than this:

•ShareaSale

•CJ Affiliate

•ClickBank

•Amazon Associates

This WordPress plugin lets you launch a fully-functioning affiliate program from start to finish in just a few minutes. You'll be able to easily track outbound links, clicks, payments, and sales from your easy-to-use dashboard, personalized to include only the data that's important to your goals.

•Track Your Results

You can use MonsterInsights to easily track the performance of your affiliate products on a WordPress site. To get started, you'll need to install and activate the MonsterInsights plugin. Then, connect your WordPress site with your Google Analytics account.

Once activated, you'll go to Insights » Settings in your WordPress dashboard and select the Tracking tab. There are several sections to the tab. We start out in the Engagement section where you can see that Enable MonsterInsights events tracking defaults to Yes, which is what we want.

Benefits Of Affiliate Marketing

Since I decided to take the plunge 5 years ago and start working for myself as an online marketer, affiliate marketing has been the best thing I ever got involved in and is now part of my daily schedule. It is without doubt something that all people who are interested in starting an online business or those who already have an online business, should investigate and take up.

If you are undecided or have little knowledge about affiliate marketing then I hope that you find the below information helpful and that it will clear up any doubts that you have over what the key benefits of affiliate marketing are.

•Commission basis

For the affiliate marketer this is a key advantage as every time that somebody makes a purchase, the affiliate receives a set commission of the profit.

For the affiliate merchant this is an advantage as they only pay the marketer when they make a sale, so no money is wasted on marketing spend.

•Huge audience

For the affiliate marketer - having built up various marketing lists or websites, they can make use of their huge audience base and ensure that the traffic they send over to the merchant is qualified and that sales are made, making the affiliate more money.

For the affiliate merchant - they receive access to a wider audience base than they may have had before, creating more interest in their products, resulting in more sales and all without investing any more money or time.

•Ease

For the affiliate marketer - once they have set up their additional sites and links across to the merchant, it is very simple to manage and often affiliates will continue to make money from sales without having done anything for months.

For the affiliate merchant - they do not have to invest time and money writing content or creating expensive images in order to promote their services/ products. Instead affiliates will apply to be a part of their programme and all the merchant need do is have many affiliates all working towards promoting their products/ services and wait for the sales to flood in.

• Steady cost

For the affiliate marketer - building on the last point, an affiliate can keep receiving commission from sales of a product or service for years, despite not doing a lot of work to promote it. You do need to invest time at the start but then you have a regular source of income coming in for the market life of the service/ product.

For the affiliate merchant - they set up all the costs so the chance to make a huge profit on sales without having spent much on marketing, is very likely. They do not have to pay their affiliates much per sale to make the business relationship worthwhile, as it tends to work best on a quantity basis so everyone is happy with the set amounts.

•Brand Visibility

For the affiliate - there is a lot to be gained reputation wise from working with a range of brands and you will find that you get a lot more work should you be able to prove that you have succeeded with others in the past.

For the affiliate merchant - they receive free brand exposure on a continual basis, which is never a bad thing. If you have many affiliates working on promoting your brand, you'll soon see a boost in search engine rankings and online sales; Amazon.com is an excellent example of where this has worked in the past.

•Outsourced expertise

For the affiliate marketer - they get the continued experience to improve and work on their methods of online marketing, investing only their time, not money.

For the affiliate merchant - they will be able to utilise all kinds of affiliates who are experts in SEM (search engine marketing) and SEO (search engine optimisation) without investing a lot of money, yet still manage to get to the top of Google rankings.

•Transparency

For the affiliate marketer - through the various affiliate programmes, it is possible to see exactly when sales are made and payment is automatic, so you do not have to worry about chasing merchants for payments.

For the affiliate merchant - they can see and manage their R.O.I (return on investment) extremely easily and do not have to worry about tracking the origin of each sale.

•Online market

For the affiliate marketer - there are an endless number of affiliate programmes out there and the demand for online shopping is not going to decrease, so the earning potential for affiliates is huge. You can access any number of markets with your affiliate work, whether you choose jewellery, hygiene, pet insurance or food.

Use long tail pro to find targeted long tail keywords with low competition, ensuring maximum affiliate sale for you.

For the affiliate merchant - as previously mentioned, online demand is not going away any time soon, therefore merchants are able to continue to expand product ranges to meet a range of online markets with the knowledge that they have a number of affiliates on hand to promote quickly and at a low cost.

•Home-based work (aimed at affiliate marketer)

If you become successful in the world of affiliate marketing then it is entirely possible to create a long term Passive Income from it and a huge bonus to this is that you can work cheaply from home and be your own boss. You don't have to pay to sign up to affiliate programmes and there are a huge number to choose from, all from the comfort of your own home.

•Overcoming tradition (aimed at affiliate merchant)

Using affiliates to promote your products and services will guarantee that you receive a lot more exposure than you would by using more pricey traditional marketing methods. Having a number of affiliates promoting what you are selling and only being paid when a sale is made, is one of the most cost effective marketing methods ever as well as being incredibly successful.

Chapter 8: Starting With Different Strategies And Ideas

Online Advertising

Online Advertising is perhaps the most straightforward approach to make cash on the web. This is obvious if you cannot seem to acquire your first latent online pay. While it is a simple concept, it is not easy in realistic terms without legal research and studying the right methods for your particular application. To make a decent pay with this promotion, it requires a great deal of traffic through your site in light of the limited quantity picked up by each snap or guest.

The absolute ideal approaches to have web-based publicity on your webpage or blog are by utilizing the accompanying:

Google **AdSense**

With Google AdSense, you can procure detached online payments from your site by creating promotions applicable to your website and its guests. An incredible aspect of AdSense is that Google does the vast majority of the difficult work for you; they discover the promoters, pick the advertisements, track the snaps, and even store the profit directly to your ledger every month. No big surprise that 65% of the best 200 sites that show promotions use AdSense.

Media.Net

Media.net is fundamentally the same as AdSense. Being Yahoo! Bing Network's response to AdSense advertisements,

Media.net is likely the second biggest logical promoting organization on the planet. They have an endorsement cycle that is somewhat broader than Google AdSense is and require a specific number of site visits a month to month to get a record with them, however once settled they can turn out a revenue stream that is fundamentally the same as AdSense.

Chitika

Chitika is like AdSense and Media.net; they are one of the mainstream elective promotion organizations and have a low payout limit. Particularly if you have a blog with less traffic, Chitika is a top-notch promotion network, which will show quality significant advertisements. If you have an excellent blog, you can anticipate a great pay from Chitika.

Affiliate Marketing

Affiliate Marketing has been around nearly as long as the web, and is an outstanding and most straightforward approach to acquiring passive income. Member promoting is essential. You bring in cash online by advancing the items or administrations of another organization and receive a paid commission on every deal you make.

The ordinary methodology accomplices up with associate projects, and practically all significant web organizations and organizations have offshoot-advertising programs. When you join and get their subsidiary connections, you can begin advancing them on the entirety of your websites.

To assemble a consistent and expanding predictable revenue stream from subsidiary displaying, you need to have traffic and advance items that have worth.

To tempt individuals to purchase those items, you need to have a page that creates relationship with your customer.

Create email supporter lists from individuals who visit your site utilizing AWeber to catch messages and react to questions. You will have the opportunity to communicate with individuals who trust you and will be more likely to do away with your proposals.

Typically, you should restrict the kinds of items to those that are firmly connected with the subject of your site or blog. Excellent partner dealer administrations include Google AdSense, Amazon Associates, ClickBank, Commission Junction, and Flex Offers. They all have a vast number of various items in a wide range of specialties, so you will have to locate some quality items to look over.

Email Marketing

To be fruitful with email displaying it is essential not to be viewed as a con artist or to overwhelm individuals with immaterial garbage mail. You will lose individuals rapidly from your mailing list if you do. However, whenever done effectively and elegantly, this can be an extremely fruitful technique for displaying and expanding the odds of more buys.

Niche Websites

Niche Websites are a sound and fruitful approach to create decent pay if you have a strong item. They can be committed to one subject. At that point, they become essential to a select number of individuals; however, individuals who are bound to buy since they are keen regarding the matter of your site. These sorts of sites or specialty sites are simpler to promote and are better for being gotten via web crawlers, conveying you straightforwardly to the correct clients.

Another approach to bring in cash from specialty destinations is to sell them by closeout at sites like Flippa. You should have an entire arrangement of specialty locales; these could be related subjects or shocking autonomous, independent subjects, all adding to your passive income. Thebest web business people, build up different sites because it expands the potential you have for making increasingly more income with each web page.

Writing Free-Lance

Individuals who are good at writing articles, sites, and short anecdotal stories can regularly discover there is a business opportunity for readymade, an excellent quality substance that they might have the option to sell on destinations like Upwork, eLance or Freelancer. Some mainstream destinations like eHow, About.com, and Yahoo are searching for essayists, and by selling or even contributing routinely to these locales it can increase your standing. Will help you with haggling for better always rates just as having the option to seek a portion of the more lucrative independent positions. A significant number of these will pay $50 every hour or more. Itis crucial to stay in touch with your customers this is particularly significant if you have a drawn-out agreement or a long-term project. By sending them regular updates, you will construct positive customer relationships. Trust in your capacities and posing inquiries guarantees you have a decent comprehension of the work required

If you have work and are thinking that, it is difficult to complete your agreement, contact the individuals you are working for at the earliest opportunity and let them know. The business will be business, and usual graciousness goes far. Individuals should be sure you can be depended on or will not utilize you again and undoubtedly decimate your standing, so never do whatever will hurt your reputation. People with knowledge of Site enhancements or SEO will discover a tremendous amount of interest in different articles written in a way that encourages the use of terms such as keywords, sentences, headers.

Advancing Clickbank items Clickbank is currently presumably the essential computerized items commercial center on the web. One of the measurers it utilizes is called 'gravity' to speak to how well an item sells, in light of the number of deals have been made and how later these deals were. Clickbank has an offshoot program where you can locate an immense scope of items. When you sign up you can advance any of your own or others' things, as to discover individuals who will move your items, so you can conceivably get immense after for your site.

Advancing Amazon Products

The Amazon offshoot program is an excellent method to advance items, either your own or other people's, through a dependable, reliable, and notable online store. Their payments are tiny, but they have a tremendous measure of traffic. You can procure a commission when you send somebody to Amazon if they purchase whatever else on within24 hours, regardless of whether they wind up purchasing the item you advanced or not. Thus, if you sent a book and the individual you directed to Amazon wound up buying something different, you will get the commission for both. This can amount to a decent additional reward.

Advancing Commission Junction Products

Commission Junction is one of the most seasoned and prominent associate organizations on the web today. The majority of their dealers are grounded, which is leeway if you are hoping to advance better brands. They offer a few alternatives, including pay for every deal offers, pay per lead offers and different sorts of requests.

DigiResults focuses on advancing Products and web advertising items; however, they additionally have different items ranging from wellbeing and wellness to travel. Merchants and partners are paid at the retail location, not a month or two later, like most commercial centers, making them more alluring.

Basic Virtual Assistant Jobs

Even though this is not passive income, as you need to invest a modest quantity of energy, these things are acceptable because you are paid for doing essential undertakings on the web.

Cashbacks

This is an extraordinary method to be compensated for buying or utilizing items you intend to purchase anyways. Cashback destinations pay you when you navigate them, go to retailers, and make purchases. There are over 2,000 stores that offer cash back, including Walmart, Target, Sears, Calvin Klein, and others. You can get a $10 gift voucher after your first $25 worth of buys.

Taking Surveys

There are many free overview sites offering clients the capacity to be paid for taking classes on the web. These destinations should be free and if you experience a review site that costs money, maintain a strategic distance from it. There are numerous acceptable locales. Investigate Global TestMarket, Mobrog or Toluna Survey Center. You will never get rich taking surveys, yet it is an intriguing method to put in a couple of inactive minutes and pay for that odd espresso.

Responding to Questions

There are countless individuals posting inquiries online, and if you are a specialist in your field, you can produce pay by addressing these inquiries. JustAnswer.com is a company that encourages you to access its expert community and represent over 20 million clients. Fightfox.com is a spot for movement specialists. They have special audits and positive critiques nearly all over the place.

Composing Reviews

Various organizations will pay you for reviews of their services, especially if you have a grounded blog or another online presence is the equivalent of a comparable area.

Focus on Your Advertisers

There is no need to approach marketers with market products that create a game plan to sell your items.

Selling eBooks

Whenever done the correct way, selling eBooks can be a significant passive income stream. When you distribute your book, it is there forever, and will merely continue selling duplicates (or in case you are fortunate, bunches of copies) for quite a long time to come. Since there are many books out there, it is frequently challenging to break into this market, and it requires some investment to compose a decent book. As a rule, it will take some time for it to begin selling and generate income, however, if you know a lot about a certain topic and love to write, technology makes it truly simple for anybody to write, alter, and independently publish your eBook for nothing. With little difficulty, you can make excellent pay with eBooks. These can sell for as little as $0.99, and as far up as to more than $100, contingent upon the interest for books of your chosen subject.

A genuinely extraordinary aspect regarding composing and publishing eBooks independently is that the many online book shops, for example, Amazon, (who are by a wide margin the greatest) just as practically all the others, will rundown sell it for you with no forthright charges. You pay the premium on deals, from deal shows and book circulation, and either store the cash or give you a check. You are also free (as you own the book) to sell and market it in some other commercial center, such as eBay, ClickBank, or through your own or companions' and website.

Selling your eBook on Amazon.

If you want to sell eBooks, Amazon is the ideal decision since they are the most significant online eBook retailer and produce around 3/4 of all eBook deals. They will give you a profit of 70% eminence for each book sold. The one concern is that the customer's do not report their email address so alerts and potential sales cannot be added to your mailing list.

Selling your eBook on your website, and selling books and other items can be rewarding. You pick up the consideration of your clients and the capacity to add them to your mailing list so you can welcome them to return to your site with the goal that you can offer them some a more significant amount of your items or administrations. This is essential for developing significant traffic, particularly individuals who have just come to you.

Online Courses

If you can compose an eBook, there is no reason you cannot write or make an online course. This is another excellent method to use your time and exertion .Numerous individuals feel that online courses are more critical than eBooks, essentially because they offer mixed media substance, for example, video and sound and not merely text. Courses generally provide help, direction and instructing.

Chapter 9: Social Media Marketing

Social Media Marketing seems to be the latest buzz word for anyone looking to increase their online presence and sales, but is Social Media Marketing (SMM) all it is cracked up to be?

S.M.M companies are now springing up all over the place these days and they are telling anyone that will listen about how incredibly important social media like Facebook twitter and YouTube are to your business but, for the average small to medium sized business, does marketing to social networks really live up to all the hype? Is spending a small fortune on hiring a SMM company really worth it? And has anyone really done their research on this before they hired someone to set up there Facebook business page? Some SMM companies are setting up things like Facebook business pages (which are free) for $600 to $1,000 or more and telling their clients that they don't need a website because Facebook is the biggest social network in the world and everybody has a Facebook account.

Now while it may be true that Facebook is the largest social network in the world and yes, Facebook's members are potential consumers, the real question is are they actually buying? Social media marketing companies are all too happy to point out the positives of social media like how many people use Facebook or how many tweets were sent out last year and how many people watch YouTube videos etc. but are you getting the full picture? I once sat next to a SMM "expert" at a business seminar who was spruiking to anyone who came within earshot about the amazing benefits of setting up a Facebook business page for small business (with him of course) and selling on Facebook. So, intrigued by the aforementioned "experts" advice I looked him up on Facebook only to find he had only 11 Facebook friends (not a good start). So being the research nut that I am, I decided to take a good look into SMM in regard to selling to see if it actually worked, who did it work for and if it did why did Social Media Marketing work for them? And should business rely so heavily on social networks for sales?

As a web developer I was constantly (and now increasingly) confronted with several social networking challenges when potential clients would say that having a website sounds good but they had a Facebook business page and had been told by various sources (the ever present yet anonymous "they") that social networks were the thing to do, but after discussing their needs it became quite clear that those potential clients didn't actually know why they needed social networks or SMM to generate online sales, They just wanted it. For small and medium sized business I always recommended building a quality website over any type of social network, why? Well it's simple really because social media is Social Media, and social Networks are Social Networks they are not business media and business networks (that would be more like LinkedIn).

I know that sounds simple but it's true and the statistics back it up. The fact is that social media marketing fails to tell you that Facebook is a social network not a search engine and despite the number of Facebook users and Google users being around the same, people don't use Facebook in the same way that they use a search engine like Google (which has around half the search engine market), Yahoo and Bing to search for business or products. They use it to keep in touch with family and friends or for news and entertainment.

In a recent study done by the IBM Institute for Business Value around 55% of all social media users stated that they do not engage with brands over social media at all and only around 23% actually purposefully use social media to interact with brands. Now out of all the people who do use social media and who do interact with brands whether purposefully or not, the majority (66%) say they need to feel a company is communicating honestly before they will interact.

How Do You Use Social Media Marketing? And Is It Even Worth Doing?

Well first of all I would say that having a well optimized website is still going to bring you far more business that social media in most cases especially if you are a small to medium sized local business because far more people are going to type in "hairdresser Port Macquarie" into a search engine like Google, Yahoo and Bing than they ever will on any Social Media Site and if you don't have a website you're missing out on all of that potential business. However despite all the (not so good) statistics I still think it is still a good idea for business to use social media just not in the same way that a lot of SMM professionals are today, Why? Because it's clearly not working in the way they claim it does.

Basically SMM Companies and Business as a whole looked at social networks like Facebook as a fresh market ripe for the picking and when Facebook started getting users measured by the millions PayPal co-founder Peter Thiel invested US$500,000 for 7% of the company (in June 2004) and since them a few venture capital firms have made investments into Facebook and in October 2007, Microsoft announced that it had purchased a 1.6% share of Facebook for $240 million. However since Facebook's humble beginnings up until now (2012) both SMM Companies and Business have failed to truly capitalise on the huge number of Facebook users online.

The truth is numbers does not equal buyers. Is it in a Social Media Marketing company's best interest to talk social networks up? Absolutely. Is it in a Social Network like Facebook's best interests for people to believe that companies can sell en masse by advertising and marketing with them? Of course it is. In early 2012, Facebook disclosed that its profits had jumped 65% to $1 billion in the previous year as its revenue which is mainly from advertising had jumped almost 90% to

$3.71 billion so clearly the concept of SMM is working out for them but it is working out for you? Well... statistically no, but that does not necessarily mean that it never will.

I believe the major difference between social networks and search engines is intent. People who use Google are deliberately searching for something so if they do a search for hairdressers that's what they are looking for at that particular time. With something like Facebook the primary intent is usually to connect with friends and family. In October 2008, Mark Zuckerberg himself said "I don't think social networks can be monetized in the same way that search (Search Engines) did... In three years from now we have to figure out what the optimum model is. But that is not our primary focus today".

One of the biggest problems business face with social networks and SMM is perception. According to the IBM Institute for Business Value study there were "significant gaps between what businesses think consumers care about and what consumers say they want from their social media interactions with companies." For example in today's society people are not just going to hand you over there recommendations, Facebook likes, comments or details without getting something back for it, so the old adage "what's in it for me?" comes into play.

So the primary reason most people give for interacting with brands or business on social media is to receive discounts, yet the brands and business themselves think the main reason people interact with them on social media is to learn about new products. For brands and business receiving discounts only ranks 12th on their list of reasons why people interact with them. Most businesses believe social media will increase advocacy, but only 38 % of consumers agree.

Companies need to find more innovative ways to connect with social media if they want to see some sort of result from it. There were some good initiatives shown in the IBM study of companies that had gotten some sort of a handle on how to use social media to their advantage, keeping in mind that when asked what they do when they interact with businesses or brands via social media, consumers list "getting discounts or coupons" and "purchasing products and services" as the top two activities, respectively a U.S ice cream company called Cold Stone Creamery offered discounts on their products on their Facebook page.

Alternatively there is a great program launched by Best Buys in the U.S called Twelpforce where employees can respond to customer's questions via Twitter. With both Cold Stone Creamery and Twelpforce the benefit is clearly in the favour of the potential customer & the great trick to social media marketing is to sell without trying to sell (or looking like your selling) unfortunately most social media marketing is focused the wrong way.

Building a tangible buyer to consumer relationship via social media is not easy and probably the most benefit to business' using social media to boost their websites Google rankings. But business' need to understand that you can't just setup a Facebook business page and hope for the best. SMM requires effort and potential customers need to see value in what you have to offer via your social media efforts give them something worth their social interaction and time and then you may get better results.

Importance of Social Media Marketing?

In the world of technology communication has become easier than ever. The world has now shrunk from a vast populated land to a network of communicating individuals living in a global village. People from all over the globe have come closer together and distances have decreased to the extent that an individual is merely a click away.

In this ever-growing network of people a new theory has emerged, the idea of 6 degrees of separation. The idea behind this is that between you and any another person in the world is only a chain no longer than six people. This emphasizes the significance of online communication and the way it has made the world a whole lot smaller.

This is the power of social media and the developments in online communication. A happening in one part of the world reaches to the second part in a matter of seconds. Imagine if that news or happening was about you. The significance of this technology is the ease it provides. Using this tool to your advantage can give you a large number of benefits.

•Social Media Marketing brings global fame to your name.

This is your ticket to international level fame. Your company or your name could be known throughout the globe with millions of followers and fans. Millions of people can access these sites where people come to communicate online and express their views. Once you step into the world of the social media marketing all of these people become your potential prospects. Your services are merely a single search away.

•Promote your business or product as a serious product.

This technology provides you access to virtually the whole world and all its inhabitants. They are there to read and share anything that you have to say. This is your chance to establish an image for yourself that "Hey! I am here to do business" and "I am serious about the product or services that I provide".

•Brings you closer to thousands of people without much effort.

Social media marketing is practically free. If you were to attempt to reach out to millions of people through physical means you would have to make a lot of investments. This technology is the way to most efficiently reach out to your potential clients, not only in terms of finances but in terms of time as well.

•Gives you feedback on the type of viewer you have.

An interesting thing about marketing on these social websites is the level of feedback that you can expect. Using social media marketing can in fact educate you about the people who are or might be interested in your product or service. This gives you a better chance of altering your campaigns to gain improved results. You may learn about the number of people who visit you page, or the ages of people who comment or share your posts, or even their ethnicities, localities, religion, hobbies and preferences. You educate the world about your product and social media marketing educates you about the people who took interest in it. You get to know them personally through the network of social media.

•Established an efficient communication channel between you and your client.

Your client may have some issue or he may need help or want to enquire more about your product. Your presence on social media allows you to respond to him on a personal level. This in turn assures the client that you are responsible and instills a sense of trust.

•Your company is seen as a person.

Generally people might not prefer to do business with a company or a corporation and prefer to work with individuals. This is because a person is real; he has a real presence in this world, he is someone you can relate to, he has feelings, thoughts, and emotions. Having your business on the social media gives it a human personification. It appears to be more of an individual than a company; someone people can talk to; someone people can reach out to. This creates a comfort zone between the clients and your company and produces benefits for both.

•Makes you more accessible.

Social media sites ensure your presence 24 hours a day, 7 days a week. You client can easily drop off a message and you can choose to reply as soon as you wish. This strengthens the bond between you and your customer and inspires a feeling of loyalty for your brand. This constant availability cannot be found when dealing with a physical office due to office opening and closing times. This ease for the customers to reach out to you in their time of need can only be ensured by social media.

•Social media levels the playing field.

Whether you are a multinational company or a single person start-up, in the world of social media you are all on the same level. Your finances and resources may not make much of a difference when it comes to social media. What does make a difference is your skill to communicate and attract people and the quality of the product or services that you provide. In the physical world, new start-ups would face immense financial difficulties in trying to promote themselves, while the marketing of giant enterprises would continue to dominate. Social media network gives you a fair playing field to show your true spirit and skill.

•You might discover new potential clients or customers.

While reviewing your feedback of viewers you might begin to see obvious patterns in your business response. People from a particular region that you might never have thought of are showing a lot of interest in your product are your best clients. These patterns will also allow you to see a certain untapped markets that you can exploit. You can swiftly move and make use of the opportunity.

•Marketing campaign is easier to manage and cost-effective.

Setting up a social media marketing campaign requires much less effort than actually setting out to physically execute you marketing campaign for example putting up banners or advertisements etc. in order to get you message across. Social media marketing is relatively easy to manage and quite frequently updated.

•Your network grows exponentially.

As more people add to your social network, they become the cause for more people to join in. As the people keep adding the rate at which people are added grows with them. And as the tree branches out, so will your business.

•People are more receptive to Social Media.

People tend to pay more attention to things on the social media. The reason being that people feel that compared to mainstream marketing social media has no political agenda behind the information or the presence of any big corporation trying to sell their products. It is just people sharing their knowledge and opinions. Therefore the people tend to pay more attention to social media posts and are more influenced by them as opposed to

155

specialized advertisements. People regularly check their social media feeds for posts that their friends and family make, and there you are, right in between all their posts with your latest news or promotion. The readers are bound to pay attention to what you have tried to communicate and then forward the news to their acquaintances and the message will spread exponentially.

Chapter 10: Making A Passive Income From A Small Budget

Making a passive income on the web is a dream for many people, yet it can turn into a reality for any individual with P.C. and web association. Regardless of whether you are merely starting to dealing with the web and wish to figure out how to generate passive income, or if you have been battling to make payments from it, there are a couple of things you ought to consider before hopping in the advanced web pool.

Some significant inquiries you ought to consider when choosing your best methodology are:

Do you have something you want to market?

Do you now have a type of essence on the web (a site, blog or web-based media accounts)?

Do you have a financial plan?

What is your web insight? What will you need to figure out to be fruitful? There are a couple of astounding approaches to begin producing a passive income without going through a ton of cash. Although it is conceivable to maintain a business without spending anything, this methodology would generally be a long cycle and require a lot of work. The best system is to build up spending you can bear and work with it. The larger sum you have in your spending plan, sensibly speaking, and the quicker and more superficial it is to arrive at a pay level that will uphold your way of life. In any case, there are numerous individuals on the net but frauds are easy to fall for, so be careful!

Getting a presence on the web can be refined by beginning via online media destinations like Facebook, Google Plus, Twitter, LinkedIn, YouTube, Pinterest, and Instagram. The issue with these locales is they are currently turning out to be packed to such an extent that the opposition is hard to adapt to and it is simple for your undertakings to lose all sense of direction in the tide of data introduced. A couple of years back these locales functioned admirably. Presently, with over 3.5 Billion individuals utilizing the web routinely, it takes a touch of skill to use them adequately.

Being particular and cautious in where you place your venture dollars is the way to start. To start, you will require a site, which could be a standard site or a blog. Numerous organizations give you platforms to dispatch and keep up your site. What you pick relies upon what you are selling, the administration you are advancing and your spending plan.

Web facilitating destinations like the free Google My Sites are decent choices. It is preferable that it is open, and the Google web indexes effortlessly find it... In any case, it accompanies restrictions.

Different destinations, like Bluehost and WordPress, are my favored alternatives. I like these destinations since they are easy to use and have a proper assistance administration, including a chat service. The Bluehost Bundle helps you get a free name for only a few dollars per month.c for example, (I will utilize my term for an example)   www.RichardGadson.com.

Additionally, you can make up to 10 sub-areas, or pages, where you can advance your items or administrations.

If you are advancing a cookbook for instance, (regardless of whether you are the writer or merely doing another writer's work) your sub-area could be OrganicCookingwithRichardGadson.com. These are convenient and can be customized to suit any application, for example, Richard@RichardGadson.com or RichardsCookbook@RichardGadson.co. It is always a good idea to utilize your name in your site. This is so there is so you will develop a brand that is clearly associated with your name. If you utilize sub-par items and do not give incentives, then you will have a short future on the web.

If you have an item that you need to sell without your name related to it, you can, in any case, utilize one of your sub-spaces and exclude your name from the web address. For instance, you may locate a superb choice of gourmet specialist's blades and make a course of action with the maker to sell them, and utilize one of your free sub-areas to do this. You may wish to make a dessert cookbook, and that could be on a subspace page of your principal website...

When you or join Bluehost and WordPress, they provide the most proficient method to set up your web site and business, alongside a heap of supportive counseling...

An aloof web pay could be accomplished by re-appropriating all the essential work and supervising the activity, yet that requires some info, so there is nothing of the sort as a passive income website. Having expressed that, it is conceivable, and entirely sensible, to have a very low upkeep pay site, mainly if you utilize and gain proficiency with a portion of the instruments and strategies accessible from your WordPress site where it is conceivable to incorporate adaptation into your WordPress site and increment the procuring capability of your locales with negligible exertion. You will have to do the entire regular, for instance, writing new posts, ads and website support, but the lucrative approach will be straightforward and needs no initiative on your part.

Making a Passive Income with a Larger Budget.

When putting resources into any lucrative venture, remember that everything is relative; the sum you can hope to procure is comparative with risk. A generally safe for the most part implies a low financing cost. A high loan fee signifies acquisition risk, of losing your speculation. The ideal approach to decide whether something can be an advantageous passive income stream is by contrasting the probable return and the current danger-free pace of profit for state and government bonds. The 10-year government bank security yield is at about 3% so endeavor you attempt should have a significantly preferable return. Otherwise, you are squandering your efforts since you can procure 3% sitting idle.

It should be noticed that various nations' legislatures set multiple rates. For instance, in the Philippines, you can get a return after assessment (the public authority retains the expense) of at any rate 7% on government securities, and the Philippine government ensures these rates. (Some would state this is somewhat unsafe; however, they have never defaulted and are a preferred danger over numerous European nations' legislatures and banks.) Therefore, I would recommend that if you do not arrive generously over 7% p.a. disregard it.

Web Share Market Investing

A large portion of us has heard how a few people make an immense fortune contributing to the securities exchange. In reality, you can make considerable monetary profits putting resources into stocks and offers. First-time financial specialists must know about before putting resources into reserves some extremely standard errors. If you have to add two to three hundred dollars to perceive what is happening, it is all right. If, though, you do not get a good passive gain, then it is a real hope that knowledge like any other will be consumed.

Do not merely bounce in carelessly, even though the details of putting are very straightforward in principle, that is, purchase low and sell high. The vast majority do not, practically speaking, in any case, understand what low and high genuinely mean. What is high to someone selling is typically viewed as low (or adequately low) to the purchaser in any exchange so that various ends can be drawn from similar data. Due to the market's general idea, it is imperative to require some investment to consider what stocks or offers are doing before bouncing in.

Before beginning, you ought to learn in any event the essential measurements, for example, book esteem, isolated yield, value income proportions, etc. See how they are determined, where their significant shortcomings lie and where these measurements have commonly been for any stock and its industry after some time.

In the beginning, simulated cash can be used in a stock test scheme or on a prototype account to help you understand how things work and save a substantial amount of money.

At the point, your first income is exciting. With a meagre $100, you can get significantly more offers in penny stocks than you could if purchasing a blue-chip stock that could cost $50 or more (some considerably more) for a recommendation. Penny stock gives a decent benefit if it goes up by a dollar. However, lamentably, what penny stocks offer in their use must be estimated against the instability they have. They are called penny stocks for a reason; generally, they are inferior quality organizations that will not work out as a beneficial arrangement. Losing 50 pennies on a penny stock could mean a 100% misfortune. Losing 50 pennies on a $50 bargain is not so awful and can typically be recovered later, given time. Getting robust data on penny stocks can be troublesome, settling on them a helpless decision for a financial specialist who is yet learning, as they are defenseless.

It is a smart thought to consider stocks in rates and not entire dollar sums. In the meantime, when you begin to handle supplies, instead of seeking to make a big buck to low performing companies, the vast majority should manage stocks, as most gains for penny stocks are karma.

Try not to be enticed to put everything in one explicit speculation; ordinarily, it is not a decent move. As can be expected, any organization has issues and sees their stocks decrease significantly. This occurred in the last monetary accident. Particularly in the beginning, it is a sound plan to purchase a small bunch of stocks, so you are less inclined to have a tremendous misfortune in case of issues. In general, good and bad times ought to try to show a practical benefit. The exercises learned while doing this at that point, become less expensive, yet meaningful.

Be cautious about getting to contribute as nothing is ever a definite wagered. If you acquire stocks, it is called utilizing your cash. This amplifies both the increases and the misfortunes on given speculation. If you have $100 to contribute and choose to get $50 to purchase $150 of a specific stock and the stock ascents 10%, you make $15, or a 15% profit for your capital. In any case, then again, if the stock decreases 10%, you would lose $15, or a 15% misfortune, however, what is imperative to comprehend is that if the stock goes up by half, you will make a 75% return which is extraordinary, in any case, if the stock decays half, you lose all the cash you acquired, and that's just the beginning. Therefore, until you have experienced, it is perceptive not to get to contribute.

It is imperative to know that you might lose every one of your speculations in one night, so it is fundamental to utilize the cash you can stand to lose. If you begin with underlying speculation and make a couple of gains, take a rate from the benefits and reinvest that. At that point, by gradually developing your all-out speculation you will be in a more grounded position without gambling excessively. Contributing should be seen as a drawn-out business, regardless of whether you are a dealer or a purchasing and holding type financial specialist. To remain in business, you need to have some money held as an afterthought for crises and openings. This money will not procure any return, however, having all your money in the market is a danger that even proficient speculators won't take if you need more money to contribute and save some for a crisis money hold, at that point you're not in a position monetarily where contributing bodes well.

The sound exhortation is elusive, and attempting to figure the following large thing or quickest developing cost, hot tips, or dealing with gossipy tidbits is not a sound field-tested strategy. It can be loaded with risks for first-time speculators. Keep in mind, you are contending with professional firms that not just get as soon as it is available, but have also had long stretches of involvement and ability to investigate it rapidly appropriately. If you are fortunate, you will win a little, but if your karma runs out, you could lose everything. The best arrangement for amateurs is to stay with interests in organizations you comprehend and have individual experience managing. You ought not to deal with contributing like playing the lotto. At the point when you are explicitly purchasing stocks, you are going up against enormous shared assets and expert financial specialists that do this full-time and will have more assets. When you initially start contributing, it is ideal to begin with little and face the challenges with the cash you are set up to lose, as the market can be unforgiving to any missteps. As you become more proficient at assessing stocks, you can begin making larger speculations.

Cash Trading Foreign Exchange Forex Trading

Forex exchanging is about the theory of the cost of one nation's money against another. Being a Forex merchant offers one of the most fantastic ways of life t, yet it is one of the least secure. However, if you are persistent, you can get it going.

It would help if you bought the EURUSD cash pair low and then (ideally) give it up for higher prices to make a profit... T currency strengthens if you buy the euro against a dollar (EURUSD) so you will be likely to fail. Therefore, it is imperative to know about the risk associated with exchanging Forex, and not just the prize. As a broker, you can either rake in cash or lose cash rapidly. The crucial thing about currency market management knows the dollar amount that puts you at risk when you enter an exchange and be ok with the losing money, since an exchange may be a washout.

Forex is the world's largest sector with a profit of over3 trillion dollars a day. Anybody can open an exchanging account with as little as $250 and start exchanging the same day. Straight through request execution permits you to exchange quickly. It has a bit of leeway over trading shares. There are fewer cash sets to zero in on, and you can exchange with anywhere on the planet with only P.C. and web association. With many retail market-producers, there is no commission and generally lower exchange costs than stocks and products. On top of that, brokers have occasions to benefit from rising or falling business sectors.

All fledglings should know that exchanging conveys both the potential for remuneration and danger. Numerous individuals come into the business sectors contemplating the prize and overlooking the risks in question. This is the best way to sacrifice the full value of your bill. If you need to begin exchanging the Forex market, study it first. Various network destinations offer free courses and can be helpful in learning about exchanges.

Chapter 11: How To Successfully Market Your Product Online

Marketing a product online can be the death of it if you are scared to do it. Some people don't even want to create a product for fear that it won't be successful. You should not let fear get in the way of you trying to reach out to people and show them what you can do for them.

Marketing your product online can be done with ease when you are familiar with the way you need to do it. There are so many ways to market your products online, but the successful ways will be determined when you find what works and you stick to it.

The first thing you must know is it takes six to eight times of your product being in front of a person before they will even consider looking at your site and making the purchase. They have to be able to trust you and they have to make sure that you are not a fly by night marketer. This is why you need to decide on a few ways to market your product and stick to it for two or three months.

Now the first way you can market your product successfully is to create an affiliate program. When you do this, you will have the help of your affiliates to promote and sell your product. You will reach out to higher levels of people using an affiliate program than you can on your own.

Another successful way to promote your product is to use button ads. A button ad is a square picture that is placed on a site and linked to your site. This means when someone clicks on the picture, it will take them to your site.

Text and link ads are also successful ways to promote your product, but you need to be careful with these. You are limited to the words in a text ad, so you want to give as much information as possible in very few words. With link ads you are restricted to your web address only, so you will need to use that wisely as well.

Social media is another successful way to promote your product. You can use websites such as Twitter.com or Facebook.com, but before not to SPAM your readers with your posts.

Promoting your products online is a great way to reach people outside of your hometown. You can reach people in all parts of the world with your website.

Using the techniques listed above will help you successfully market your product online using your website.

Conclusion

I trust that I have offered you some pragmatic insights on various approaches to creating passive revenues on your long-term retirement. By investigating your circumstances and checking whether there are any areas in which you can improve your financials, by definition, passive income is where you do work to give a resource that you can profit from. A few people have land that they use to gather rentals or purchase item and sell at a higher price, others put their cash in stocks or bonds and live off the returns. Individuals who do not have the funding to make a huge venture that will support a way of life they wish to have, they should utilize different alternatives, such as making or composing eBooks. This can speak to an enormous interest when the same number of eBooks require months or years to compose. This kind of venture can pay off as the book can continue selling for a long time.

Normally the individuals who are effective at acquiring long-term passive income do so via cautious arranging and spreading their assets out. This will diminish the odds of any misfortunes and expand the odds of picking up a superior pay from your benefit base. The well-known axiom 'don't keep all your investments tied up in one place' is shrewd. Numerous financial specialists have come unraveled because they put resources into just a single zone and could not assimilate the misfortunes they brought about. Spending over your absolute limit or not considering the need to support and keep up your web presence should be evaded. Yet, good judgment and thinking ahead can go far to forestalling most issues.